# The Return to Việt Nam

## by Jade Hidle

TRANSCURRENT

t

2016

To my mother-Mẹ, for everything.

In memory of my grandmother-Bà Ngoại, Chanh Thi Hoffman, the warrior who brought all of us here. Thank you for teaching me how to transcend language through sharing meals, laughing, dancing silly, and always fighting for a better life.

# The Return to Việt Nam

## ACKNOWLEDGEMENTS

Coeditors: Michael Buckley and Jason G. Casem

Layout and design: Jason G. Casem

Biography photograph by: Chad Tsuyuki

# TABLE OF CONTENTS

## Foreword

Jade Hidle's exploration of her identity construction is another testament of the North-American ethnic impulse to shore up biracial desires that proclaim one's uniqueness and, more importantly, one's sense of self—a fluid dynamism to be a part of and apart from two cultures that promise recognition and acceptance. Each piece in this collection showcases Hidle's talent as she skillfully threads the fictional and nonfictional narratives of her culture's past and present through her own personal pursuit to define what it means to be a Vietnamese American woman.

The raw and unrefined reality exemplified in Hidle's essays and storytelling illustrates an intoxicating mixture of fear and desire, as her voice pulls the reader through her maturation from childhood, adolescence, and into a matured woman's return to her mother's homeland nearly 8,000 miles away from Southern California. As depicted in her narratives, the life and enculturation of a young Vietnamese American girl, living in a 20th-century San Pedro housing project, demands multiple and, often times, warring or competing sets of gender performances that reward, punish, or ridicule Hidle for conforming to or digressing from what her friends, childhood bullies, and matriarchy deem necessary and worthy for her position in society—a position that is constantly depicted straddling the threshold of acceptance and belonging.

Now it is that threshold in Hidle's work that fixes and fascinates me, and it is best demonstrated in "Body-Borderland." The moments in which she precisely recognizes and articulates the "phantom past-future movements" that haunt and, at times, frustrate her sense of belonging are the moments where I too feel this phantom state lurking beyond her words on the page and proceed to overwhelm the calculations in my mind and penetrate my heart. As she listens to a young Vietnamese woman express her hopes for something much greater than working in a Sài Gòn massage parlor, Hidle awakens and conjures the phantasmal presences that she has inherited:

> I am saddened by what my language has unlocked. And I am ashamed to admit that I felt I had no other option than to empty [my wallet] into her . . . hands. 'Save for school,' I tell her, 'and get out of this place.' The boss lady watches us suspiciously from behind the counter.

The shame Hidle reveals is sharp and poignant; the weight of its confessional tone is the spirit of a liminal being depicted standing at the center of a threshold, crossing, or borderline, attempting to simultaneously define and redefine existence—an existence cultural and gender theorist Gloria E. Anzaldúa describes in *Boderlands/La Frontera*:

> Borders are set up to define the places that are safe and unsafe, to distinguish us from them. A border is a dividing line, a narrow strip along a steep edge. A borderland is a vague and undetermined place created by the emotional residue of an unnatural boundary. It is in a constant state of transition.

Hidle's acute sense of awareness repeatedly negotiates and traverses the "constant state of transition" that Anzaldúa identifies.

As a master storyteller, Jade Hidle pushes my consciousness into an unsafe space; her brilliance pricks and releases the "emotional residue" besmeared over the deep and faraway things hidden in my heart.


Jason G. Casem

July 31, 2015

# Part One: U.S.-Việt Nam

In the days before I go back to Việt Nam, and I say "go back" even though I had only ever been there through stories, my mother stuffs granola bars and rolls of toilet paper into my suitcase, warning me not to tell anyone that I am Vietnamese. She warns that if they find out, whoever "they" are, they will harass me for money, call my mother a traitor, find out where my Saigonese family lives and do unspeakable things. These dangers are the main reason that my mother does not want to accompany me to her country of birth. She wants me to let them continue to think that I am a tourist and only a tourist. You can speak Vietnamese to them, she says, but say that you learned it at school, that you are just there for the cheap food and beaches. "Be American," she says in the way that is soft and safe and nice, whereas she sometimes spits this word at me as if it is a dirty word. "Only eat clean food," she reminds me, "otherwise you be sick." I haven't told her that in the weeks leading up to the trip, I broke my decade-long vegetarian diet to eat fish and chicken because I could not bear to refuse these meat dishes if they were offered to me by impoverished hands. I'd begun to feel guilty for my nasty American privilege of denying certain foods for dietary purposes or political principle, while my relatives from the other side of the Pacific had to eat anything, everything they could find. "Most important," my mother interjects, "don't look at anyone in the eye too long. You know we don't like that."

Though her worries and warnings make me feel unsafe within my own skin, I know I will not abide by what my mother says. I will be a bad daughter. I will tell everyone that I am Vietnamese and I won't wipe down silverware before eating with it and I will look into people's eyes to see if I can find home there, because I need to feel that I am going home.

# For My Mother

I was four years old, and my mother was gone for what felt like days at a time for nursing school internships, and elsewhere. Though my grandmother was charged with supervising me, she was functioning on Việt Nam time—smoking, gambling, napping, smoking, disappearing, returning. So, I structured my days myself: *He-Man*, reading, crawling onto countertops to reach cupboarded food, forcing Barbies to survive imagined natural disasters of pillow avalanches and bathtub floods, more microwaved canned food, reading, *Alf, Small Wonder*.

The momentum of these repeated structures would mount in anticipation of my mother's return. Upon one of her many returns, my legs—clothed, I remember clearly, in red stretch pants—hung off of the bed we shared and kicked into a run toward her as soon as she opened the door. "Mẹ ơi, mẹ ơi" I called to her. She cupped one side of my face with one hand, and pushed my other cheek to her face so she could inhale sharply, quickly, deeply in a Vietnamese mother's kiss. "Cái gì, con?" she asked. I imagine now that she was maybe a little alarmed at the urgency of my greeting her upon her arrival. I was usually more withholding. I had learned to be more cautious of her when she returned so as to gauge her emotions. But, this time, I had a story to tell her, one that could not wait.

I do not remember now what the story was, nor do I think it matters. The part of the memory that matters is that, in that hopeful moment of reunion with my mother, I struggled to articulate the story I wanted to tell her because my body was distracted with the urgent, pressing need to defecate. I grabbed her hands, then held her face, buried my face in her tufts of her permed and teased '80s mane, my lips sputtering next to her ear as I pinched, squirmed, danced. "What the matter you?" she asked. Desperate, I tried to focus all that I had learned about control in four years of life and to send all of that knowledge directly to my butt muscles. "Mẹ," I told her, "I need to poop."

"Đi đi! Go!"

"But I need to tell you the story."

"Go first. Tell later."

"But what if I forget?"

"Forget? How long take you poop?"

"I'll hold it. I have to tell you this story."

But only slow surrender.

I soon felt the seat of my red stretch pants drop heavy and hot. I froze. My mother felt my body, once hers, tense, and she patted the back of my pants. As soon as she felt the weight there, she pulled away from me, shrieked "Gê quá!" and began to laugh.

In this moment I became acutely aware of my body—its tightness, its failures, a push from within, outward—and my revulsion with it is still tangled up in my need to tell stories. More so, I became attuned to my mother's teeth. They were straight and white in the way that only "worked-on" teeth can be. I realized then how rare it was to glimpse my mother's teeth, the ones that had been worked on over and over again from the rot of malnutrition and lack of dental care in Việt Nam, because she so seldom smiled and all of the photos she chooses to display of herself show her as a tight-lipped, controlled sort of beauty.

My mother was sad long before she was my mother, maybe always. This is not the kind of sadness that you see on the commercials for pills whose side effects may cause diarrhea and death; this is the kind of sadness of history. And she has often been that sadness more than she ever has been my mother. The things that made her sad were sights and smells and tastes that I could seize in flashes, but things that I had never experienced for myself or could never understand, let alone talk to her about. I wonder how much I have inherited this.

11

As quickly as she began to laugh, her face turned and she began to yell about me no longer being a baby and how tired she was of cleaning up other people's shit all day long. When my mother gets angry, it fills all of the surrounding space so that you breathe it and taste it, and I want to hold on to her smile, those teeth, her laughter until it expands in me so that I fill the room and can push all of the anger out. But that doesn't work because I am only me, and so I learned to clean up my own shit very early on.

This was the reunion that made visible to me that my mother and I were always-already two different people, two different bodies bearing so many different memories. Every story I've told since is bound up in the feeling of the hot messiness of being too close to myself and too far from all that is my mother, of feeling that I am divulging secret traumas that are at once mine yet always a stranger's.

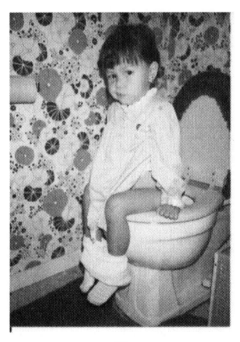

## Part Two: Life-Death in the Pacific

"It is said that the sea is history."—Saidiya Hartman

With my forehead pressed against the airplane window, the ocean appears a placid, open space that extends empty for miles and hours, but I know it is full with history, ghosts.

Some of my uncles who tried to escape by boat were captured and beaten before they even made it to the water and had to wait until the '80s and '90s to immigrate to the U.S. They never spoke about it, though. When I asked one of my uncles about it, he only laughed and showed me his purpled gums where false teeth had been inserted to replace the ones that had been knocked out.

My stepfather, who made it to a boat, once told, in unsettlingly nonchalant fashion, the story of the journey—drinking urine, escaping Thai pirates, sunburned lips, beatings, arriving alive on unfamiliar shores. "Florida real nice," he says to end the story, as if it were a vacation.

Around the same time but on the other side of the Pacific, my biological father was surfing waves, his Irish-Norwegian skin freckling in the California sun, because his birthday was selected as 324th out of the 365 days of the year for the draft. My dad once told me a story that he said I would think was funny. Fresh out of college, he interviewed for a job at a bank, where the hiring committee asked him, "What do you think of the war in Vietnam?" In his telling of this story, it is at this moment that my dad pauses and shrugs, his Jesus-translucent green eyes searching the sky, before he tells me what he told the bankers: "You know, I'd never really thought about it." I wait for something else to follow. "I didn't get the job," my dad explains to me, as if this is my concern. "So don't ever say that in a job interview," he adds with an embarrassed laugh. I am struck silent by the dissonance of my mother and father's respective stories. What was my mother going through in Việt Nam at the time that my dad was shrugging through his interview? Was she living one of the stories she recited to me throughout my childhood? The one in which gunfire suddenly sprayed across the open-air market and all she, and I, could remember was the vision of the dragonfruit clutched in a dead neighbor's hand, before her survival instinct took over and she shimmied through an irrigation ditch all the way to her grandmother's house? Was it the week of enforced curfew during which she resorted to eating bugs that crawled into the house? Or the time she was at the lake in Đa Lat and Phật Bà appeared to her in the sky? "She look so real," my mother had told me once as she kneeled at her altar. Through her story, I could feel the thickness of humid air and the rippling heat waves giving texture to Phật Bà's robe.

These memories, at once mine and not mine, cycle through my mind as I listen to Vietnamese families on the plane bicker about sharing the armrests, as I study the flawless skin and lips of the Taiwanese airline's flight attendants, and mostly as I gaze out of the airplane window while everyone watches in-flight movies or sleeps. The ocean below is always all of these stories—their dissonance and their complement.

# Ghosts

Growing up, I believed in ghosts, without doubt. My mom told me stories about the ghosts she encountered in Việt Nam, always stressing that there was more death and haunting there than I, having been born in the U.S., could ever know. She told me of the little girl floating in the bathroom in my mom's house in Nha Trang. My mom was home alone and went to the bathroom and found the girl there, floating cross-legged. When she saw my mother, she opened her mouth and a long, sharp tongue unrolled, lapping at my mother, who passed out and was later found by my grandmother.

I spent much of my childhood at my grandparents' house in San Pedro, where I became attuned to the invisibles:

In my uncle's bedroom where he used to pop the screen off the window to shoot crows off of the telephone wires running above the backyard, the glass on the windows and sliding glass doors frosted in the middle of the day and books fell off the shelves onto my head.

In my auntie's room, lights turned on and off in the closet, and when I slept in that room while she was out with her friends, I often woke up on the floor or with the sheets tied around my ankles.

In the living room, I once suddenly fell off a chair and broke my arm. When I tried to sit up, my whole body was held down by a great weight. I could not move any part of my body until my grandma came home to me lying flat on the floor. "What you do?" she asked.

And always, always, when I walked through the hallway that connected these rooms, I felt the weight of some force following me, hovering behind my right shoulder. I never turned to acknowledge it and pretended as best I could that I wasn't scared—I'd clutch my books or dolls or whatever toys I had with me and walk, chin forward, down that hallway, though my little heart pounded in my

16

chest. This is how I deal with fear and adversity to this day.

In this haunted house, I was left alone a lot. Grandpa would work as a handyman always in a white Dickies carpenter jumpsuit; in a cloud of cheap perfume Grandma would shuffle off to the casinos with her "boom boom, so beauty" hair, as she called it, patting the heavily Aquanetted tufts; my aunt and uncle were teenagers, watching MTV (back when the channel actually played music videos) or popping each other's bacne; and my mom would intern long hours as a nursing student and also go on dates to try to live her '20s the best she could.

So, I was left to my own devices, finding my own ways to stay safe from the invisibles. The most important aspect of creating a sense of safety was enclosing space so I could see every corner and always have my back against something solid so that I wouldn't risk feeling that spirit hovering at my back. I achieved this by taking over the space under the dining room table. We never used it, only ate together on Thanksgiving, but peeking beneath the dusty table cloth, I had a good vantage point of the kitchen, as well as the living room and the doors leading out to the backyard. I piled pillows and dolls and lots and lots of books against the chair legs on one side of the table so they always had my back. It was in this fortress that I felt the safest. I felt invisible in a powerful way, though looking back now I'm sure they knew I was there and indulged me by pretending they didn't.

From my spot beneath the dining room table, I observed my grandma as she exercised on the back porch. For my grandma, exercise started with her toenails clicking across the floor as she shuffled to the doors leading to the backyard, usually in the afternoon because she'd been up late the casinos. My grandma's toenails resemble primitive weapons cased in glass at some anthropology museum, except for the fact that they are painted in the fruity colors of Wet 'n Wild 99-cents-a-bottle nail polish. She then lit a cigarette, which she let dangle from lips James Dean-style. Then, she began to swing her arms, but never vigorously enough to destabilize that precariously balanced cigarette that glowed with each of her inhalations. At a rhythm a beat faster than the swing of her arms, my grandma's legs shook, sending her whole body into a gentle jiggle. Punctuating these synchronized, controlled tremblings of the body were the warbles of my grandma's mimicked croons of the Vietnamese operas she watched in *Paris by Night* variety shows.

A spectator in my own home, I began to push the boundaries of, and grow increasingly arrogant about, what I could get away with and what I could witness, as children often do in defining their worlds, their selves. First, I started popping my grandmother's Sucrets—the menthol burn of these purloined cough drops invigorating my little body, propelling me to more adventurous pursuits.

I began running reconnaissance missions, crawling out from under the table and slinking along the walls. Once, I saw my grandparents kiss. This might not seem like a momentous occasion, but my grandparents' relationship was defined by constant yelling (he in his George Washington voice and her in Vietnamese curses and tongue clicks. Once they even started throwing chairs at each other, which I thought meant they were really strong because I had been conquered by one of those heavy chairs. (I had tried to slip out of that chair backwards and got my head stuck between the chair back and the seat. I began to panic and cry, until my grandpa came in and just turned my head. It was a proud moment for an immigrant family.)

When I saw them kiss, it was Mother's Day 1988 and he had brought her yellow flowers, and she leaned over and kissed him. That is the only time I ever saw my grandparents exchange any measure of affection. And I, with my back against the wall, crouching behind a table, was the only one who witnessed that moment of love. No one noticed me, as far as I could tell. I became my own kind of ghost in this house.

As I became more adept at my ghostly sneaking around, I ventured toward the coffee table that had cabinets built into it. The cabinet doors bore wood carvings of ancient Chinese battles. I had seen my grandma stop at these cabinets on her way to her exercises, but I never knew what was in there because I didn't want to give away my hideout.

So, one day, as my grandma was "working out," I bellied across the floor military-style to one of the cabinets. My grandma was humming opera so I could tell, like an echolocation, that she was still on the porch. The hairs in the Confucian-style beards of the warriors carved in the door felt smooth against my little fingertips. Inside, I found packages of dried seaweed snacks, cigarettes, gold jewelry, medicines, more cigarettes, and then a book. It was a children's primer from Việt Nam. I had lots of books, but none in Vietnamese. I opened it and read the words I knew, and struggled to mouth the words that I hadn't ever seen in print, as the majority of Vietnamese I know I learned through oral storytelling and eavesdropping.

Concentrating on mouthing these sounds that were at once unfamiliar and so much like home, I had stopped listening for my grandma's humming, and hadn't realized that it had stopped. And, as attuned as I had become for sensing the invisibles and become one myself, I was so engrossed in the book that I didn't realize my grandma was standing above me, her hot pink pointy toenails directed right at me. I looked up and she asked for the book, "Gimme dat." I protested, claiming that I needed to learn more Vietnamese and that "this is a kid's book," I told her. And that's when she got mad. My grandma's eyes sharpened. I hadn't yet seen her look so serious. Usually when she saw me she did the little "miệng chu" face. "My book, how dare you steal from me." This was the tone of voice her arguments with my grandpa started with. "But, grandma—" And she raised her hand, and that space between us grew thick. I handed the book back to her. She opened it and sat on the edge of the couch, dismissing me. As I turned, I saw her mouth working in silent struggle over the letters and diacritics on the page. That's when I realized that my grandma—the woman who never lost an argument, who was sly at the casino, who could tell the dirtiest jokes I've ever heard, who smoked cigarettes cooler than any one on TV, who had fought her own wars to bring us all here—was struggling to read.

That was the moment that I confronted a different kind of ghost in the house.

Chad Tsuyuki

# Part Three: Tourist-Native

At the Sài Gòn airport, an American-born Vietnamese girl ahead of me in the customs line is taken aside. She looks full Vietnamese, not mixed like me, and I hear the customs officer call her by the Vietnamese name on her U.S. passport. But she carries her shoulders and flips her hair and moves her hands in the way that American girls do. They ask her why she is here, why her family left, if she has any family still living in the country, and what she is bringing to them. I recall my mother's story of how, upon her first return to Việt Nam in over thirty years, customs officials shook her down for money, calling her "Việt Kieu" and criticizing her "American" hair and clothing until she, burned by guilt and shame, paid them off. As I watch the girl in front of me tremble as she searches through her purse for travel documents as the customs official barks at her to hurry up, I recall the urgency of my mother's insistence that I do not reveal my "Vietnameseness" to anyone.

When I approach the customs desk, I smile as I never do in America, so widely that my teeth and gums show in the absence of my hand shielding them. My smile is my father's, which before him belonged to his mother, who with her red curls and green eyes was a poster Irish farmgirl. I feel that if I smile my Irish grandmother's smile, the customs official will not recognize the Vietnamese in me and take my Norwegian last name as affirmation that I am just an American and should pass through without trouble. And, after the official looks at my name and my face and then back at my name, I do. Relieved, I pass through and the sounds of the other official bickering with the Vietnamese American girl grow faint.

# Speak and Silence

Back in my elementary school years in San Pedro, I wanted to be friends with Ana, a dark-skinned Mexican girl with a hairdo like John Stamos circa 1987. Always, her brow was furrowed and her eyes were narrowed into a piercing perma-glare, which was probably appealing at some sub-conscious level because it reminded me of my mom.

Like me, Ana wore knock-off cartoon character t-shirts—uncharacteristically plump Mickeys of an orange that was not Earthly, let alone mousely, and Smurfs that were audaciously purple instead of blue. In these ways, Ana was familiar, but she had a strength that was different, admirable. See, no one fucked with Ana. Her Spanish cut through lines for blacktop recess games and shut shit-talking pre-pubescent boys down. More importantly, it bound her to a group of loyal girls who could switch between Spanish and English just as effortlessly, while I had no friends to whom I could whisper secrets in Vietnamese. Ana was one of the many Chicanas I wanted to be.

I don't remember what, if anything, I did to make Ana hate me. Looking back at our years of elementary school, though, I would say that her aversion to me is something much deeper rooted than the two of us and any tetherball court or lunch line disputes we may have had.

One afternoon, our class was lining up at the end of recess, and Ana was whispering in Spanish to her friend Luz. Now, to this day, I think Spanish is the most beautiful language in the world. (The first rule on the cheat sheet to my heart? Simply state the most mundane of words to induce amorous heart palpitations: Leche. Baño. Toronja.) Hearing Spanish melts away the shell of hyper-awareness that usually dictates my comportment, the one that has been cultivated through a lifetime of being told that I am too big-bodied too white, too tall, too American, and, on the reverse, so exotic, so "cute like a China doll," so different, so unplaceable.

So, with this in mind, it very well could be that due to the radiating vibrations of their Spanish conversation I had let my bodily guard down and was leaning into their conversation in attempt to catch a word I recognized or learn a new sound. Probably too closely. Probably doing something a little creepy like trying to pantomime roll my tongue as they said their "r"s.

Ana swiveled on the heels of her high-top Reeboks to face me, that glare of hers sharp and hard, and spit Spanish at me. All I caught was "pinche gordita."

I palmed my belly as if to protect its Hostess cakes-fullness from her words. The rotundity of hers mirrored mine. We were, after all, only seven and still awkward from baby fat, but this made me feel really bad and my face must have shown it because Luz—who, by the way, must've been weighing in at a good 120 by then—pulled the lollipop from her mouth and laughed until the mole on her upper lip danced its own independent jig of mockery.

Behind me in line, Jesus, who was always pulling out his baby teeth in class, had overheard Ana and rested his sweaty chin on my shoulder and said, "oh sheeeeeet!" This curse word, of course, made other second grade ears perk up and suddenly my classmates were watching, including a blond-haired, blue-eyed boy that I had loved sincerely since the first day of kindergarten. Pleased, Ana ran a hand through her Stamos-caliber pompa-mullet.

I looked to our teacher, who was across the blacktop with a janitor trying to retrieve a sobbing Conrad's shoe from on top of the kickball backstop cage. Because Conrad was about half the size of everyone else in the class, I'd had plenty of opportunities to see how long his tantrums lasted, so I knew I had time to spare in this line with Ana. My heart beat into the galloping nervousness of preparing to *do* something. "Oh yeah?" I said. "Well," and here I jutted my chin toward Ana, "May ăn cức đi!" For a second, I'm stoked by the sound of this, of how I made those "c"s cut through the air nasty-like, hoping that it sounded half as good as Spanish did. But then I remembered that all this translates to is, "You, go eat poop."

I assure you that even at seven I knew far more vulgar curses because my grandma, straight gangsta that she is, could shame Lil Wayne because her Vietnamese comes with a thousand ways to cuss out bitches. But, having been the only Vietnamese student in the class, I was hoping that my phrase's newness to my classmates' ears would sound badass or that, at the very least, I would gain some street cred with Ana for being a bilingual hermana, and she would announce "Viva La Raza!" and we, fists raised in revolutionary spirit, would march off the school grounds to freedom from all that oppressed us.

Ana, though she did not understand the words I had said, only laughed, her head tilting back to where I could see the sun glint off the beads of sweat along the line where her formidable hair met her forehead. Behind her, Luz's body quaked with guffaws and she shook her half-sucked lollipop at me. "That's a good one, Chino," she said.

Scratching his head, Jesus asked me, "Why did you call her a "cook"? Hey, Ana, you know how to cook? Why's that bad? I like spaghetti."

As they laughed, I hated them. I hated the words I had uttered. More, I hated myself for speaking my mother's language, our language, where no one would hear—the tongue that had soothed me when I was sick, that had scolded me, that reminded me of lessons that English could not, that taught me histories of blood, that taught me to name the world: its foods, its spirits, and the sea that bound me to people I'd never met.

Twenty years later, I am still struggling to learn the whens and wheres of silence.

# Part Four: Body-Borderland

Gloria Anzaldúa described the borderland as "a vague and undetermined place created by the emotional residue of an unnatural boundary. It is in a constant state of transition. The prohibited and forbidden are its inhabitants. Los atravesados live here: the squint-eyed, the perverse, the queer, the troublesome, the mongrel, the mulato, the half-breed, the half-dead." As a mixed-race Vietnamese, I live in the borderlands. The borderland wounds most deeply in the eyes of the Vietnamese, their sideways gazes in curiosity or criticism, or in their choice to completely ignore me to avoid the history that I make visible. The borderland is in the spectrum of responses I get to my mixed-race face, *their* language that comes out of *my* mouth, these poles between which I am always shuttling or being pushed. The borderland is always shifting, always following me.

My grandmother, with whom at least seventy-five percent of our conversations have been in Vietnamese, acts surprised every time I utter a Vietnamese word. Her eyes widen, she laughs, and tells me I entertain her, as if by speaking our language I've performed some kind of trick. Many people in Việt Nam push me out like this, with eyebrows raised in surprise or eyes glaring with offense, and I have to push back with the insistence that I do belong, that this is my language too—the one with which my mother welcomed me into this world.

As I walk around Sài Gòn, people grab my arms with calls in the ghosts of French colonialism: "Madame, Madame!" then followed with measured yet broken English gesturing to sandals or handicrafts or jewelry, "You like buy? What you size?" Disobeying my mother, I always respond in Vietnamese. When I speak Vietnamese, I watch their faces scan by own, calculating age and timelines in their heads. A few gray hairs. Fall of Sài Gòn. But no wrinkles yet. Orderly Departure Program. Too young. Maybe the Amerasian Homecoming

Act. In this quick moment when they realize I cannot be easily indexed, they almost always ask the fateful question: Bố em là ngừời lính, ha?/So your father was a solider? In other words, was my mother a prostitute?

This is the thrust against history. The U.S., France, Japan, China, all the way back to the *Tale of Kieu*, the epic poem that narrates a young Vietnamese girl's rape and descent into prostitution. It is Việt Nam's national allegory for centuries of rape by imperialist powers. Though I have not experienced any of these invasions firsthand, I do feel in my body the phantom past-future movements of holding each of my uncles' teeth between my fingers to place them back in the cradle of gums emptied by Viet Cong batons; to resensitize the skin that scars have numbed; to press my lips to their temples and suck out the bullets with hunger and revulsion; to make the disappeared here again so that they are more than their photographs and not the other way around.

Despite all of this history I have inherited, I remain silent when they imply that I am the product of sex in a Sài Gòn bar. I do not want to argue with their memory of history. After all, that story is true for many, including my grandmother. But I cannot answer for her. With this question, the conversation begins and ends.

However, when others, mostly Vietnamese born after the war, find out that I understand and speak the language, they will confess their life stories—all at once and uninterrupted.

On my last night in Sài Gòn , my mother's country has left me exhausted and homesick for burritos, the sound of Spanglish, and traffic lights. While trudging back to the hotel, my traveling partner tugs my arm in the direction of a late night massage parlor. Through the glass storefront, I can see the standard business's Buddha altar and a girl with a mean face in a turquoise halter top and cut-off shorts. "Are you fucking kidding me," I ask. "I'm not contributing to this shit."

"Come on," he prods. "You don't have to get a massage. Just sit there and maybe you can talk to the masseuses." I look back at the mean-faced girl who is counting money at the front counter.

The hotel is still blocks away and I do not want to walk alone, not because of the city, but because I have always felt unsafe in my own skin, so I agree to go in with him and sit. He has, though, surreptitiously signaled to the girl that he is paying for a massage for me as well.

As we are ushered down the hallway, I peer through the slivers of glass in doorways and catch glimpses of naked men stretched out under the blue light of wall-mounted televisions. One wears a heavy gold pinky ring on a hand that rests on a bulbous belly. Once we are in the back room where we are instructed to change into linen shorts and sandals, I tell Chad, "I can't do this. This is like a bad, dirty dream."

"Just relax, okay? Not everything is the whorehouse you think it is." I think of the placard in our hotel room that reads, "Do not bring the harlot into the room."

Upstairs, a weak fan blows and the television is set to the World Cup, which has kept tourists erupting into cheers in every restaurant and bar across the city for the past two weeks. My body is tense and I hold back tears as skinny man comes into place cucumbers over our eyes and some kind of cooling salve over the rest of our faces.

After he has prepped us, I hear the masseuses enter—a young man for me, and a young woman for Chad. Without saying anything to us beyond "okay?" and telling me in broken English to relax my tense muscles, the two begin massaging our legs and then place our feet in buckets of hot water as they move up to arms and shoulders. For an hour, my eyelids are weighted shut by the cucumber slices and so I only listen to these two young masseuses talk about their lives. Mostly, the girl confesses her frustration with the boss woman who does not intervene when male customers demand that she go beyond

30

what she is paid to do. The boy, like an elder brother, supports her by agreeing with the injustice of the situation. He tells her that she does not need to do what she does not want to do but that she should stay with the job so she can concentrate on saving money to go to school.

At the end of the massage and of the girl's stories, the young man peels the cucumber slices from my face and wipes it clean. Once my face is dry, he hovers over me for a moment and we look at each other for the first time. When he smiles at me, his teeth are crooked and browning. He turns to his masseuse partner and says, "This one looks a little Vietnamese, doesn't she?"

"Mmm," she agrees. "But I like this brother here," she lifts her chin to point at Chad. "His nose is straight and high, not like my flat one."

"Yes, he's very handsome," the male masseuse says. Then he turns back to me, and I feel nervous. "Do you think she understands us?"

I stammer, in Vietnamese, "Yes, I do. I understand everything you said."

Surprised, the girl stumbles backward, and one of her feet gets stuck in the bucket of now lukewarm water. Like something out of the opening credits to *Benny Hill,* she falls backward onto a tattered velvet ottoman, and the bucket lifts into the air, spilling foot water everywhere. We all laugh in this moment, but once we help her to right herself, she stares at me with seriousness in her eyes. "Chi biết nói tiến Việt, ha?"

"Da," I assure her that my Vietnamese is not merely some parlor trick. "I am Vietnamese. My mother is from Đa Lat."

"You came back," she says.

And then she tells me where she grew up, how her body looks much like it did before puberty, how she hates her nose, how her mom is always harping on her, how she likes to go shopping for shoes, how massage therapy school was her best option but all she wants is to go to college. She shows me the knots on her delicate hands and tells me that this is not the worst of it. Her hands bleed, and her partner echoes this pain, and all she wants to do is go to school. School, school, she says. I listen and Chad sits, not understanding. She asks me about what I do, and her eyes well with longing when I tell her I am a teacher. She asks me about where I live, and she asks me if Chad is married. "I want to come live with you! Then I can go to school!"

I am saddened by what my language has unlocked. And I am ashamed to admit that I felt I had no other option than to empty both my and Chad's wallets into her and her partner's knotted hands. "Save for school," I tell her, "and get out of this place." The boss lady watches us suspiciously from behind the counter. "When you come back," the girl says, clasping my hands with her own, "don't forget to come visit us."

"Yes, older sister," her partner says to me. "We'll show you what Việt Nam really is."

# Nước

on which the boat bobs and rolls and splinters. Rising on crests of waves, the boat's deck meets the early summer sun. The captain, a man with a face leathered from years of fishing, opens the hatch. He leans his wrinkled brown face into the hull and tells the huddled bodies there, "We have reached international waters." With the help of the fisherman's strong arms, the passengers ascend from the dark heat of the hull. On deck, these people maintain their clustered formation. Binh pulls away from them and leans over the lip of decaying wood at the bow. There is no hazy shape of his country in the distance. He sees dolphins gliding alongside the boat but does not tell the unfamiliar faces on board. Instead, he watches a smooth gray back arc to the surface before disappearing below again. Binh wonders if there are sharks in these waters, wonders what he cannot see. He is alone.

The dark-skinned boy with whom he went to war was killed in Sài Gòn. His friend's blood, Binh remembered, gurgled from his stomach wound like water at a rapid boil. He missed his mother. He had not seen or smelled her in three years. She existed for him only in memory and in the faded picture he kept pinned inside the breast of his shirt. Binh rested his hand on his friend's stomach until the boy died. Blood stayed crusted under his nails for weeks as he crept through jungle and marsh until he reached Mũi Né, one hundred miles north of Sài Gòn. At the fishing village, Binh traded in his guns and the đồng he had stolen from the men he had killed for a space on a boat that would leave at night, its passengers concealed and its fishing poles displayed.

The dolphins fall from view. Binh looks over his shoulder at the people who have now dispersed across the deck. Their faces are alien to him. These people—some elderly villagers, some children, others the pregnant girlfriends of American GIs full of promises—have not spoken to him. Binh cannot tell if it was out of reverence or shame that he was a soldier. A woman with dark hair and light skin sews a Japanese flag. Her hands are thin. A dark girl with the face of a pig watches the light-skinned woman and sips cháo with unblinking eyes.

Before last night's departure, Binh sat in the kitchen of the fisherman, waiting for darkness with the others. While the fisherman stood watch at the window, his daughter knelt next to a pot of cháo heating over the fire pit dug into the concrete floor. Binh's legs had fallen asleep from squatting on the hard surface, so he pulled them to his chest as he watched the girl stir the cháo, a southern Vietnamese flag wrapped around her bicep like she was a proud soldier. Her white dress pooled around her still body, only her fingers seemed to move as the flames and smoke lapped at them. Binh's legs tingled.

The fisherman strides up to Binh at the bow. The older man leans next to him silently for a moment, searching. Binh scans the empty horizon, pretending to have purpose. And then the fisherman tells him, "You are no longer bound." He pulls the line on his fishing pole taut. "There is no reason," the fisherman says," for you not to find yourself in different waters." He hands the pole to Binh. "Let me show you how to fish."

Feeling the man's strong hand pat his back, Binh misses his mother again. Last night as he lowered himself into the crowded hull, he looked up to see the fisherman's daughter on the shore, her white dress flowing in the steady night wind. She had pulled the flag from her arm and was waving it above her head. The curve of her small bicep looked silver and wet in the moonlight.

Binh casts the line into the water.

~

In their new home, Cam bounces her baby on her lap as Robert clears his writings off his desk. In the center of the table, he places a stack of forms whose words are typed clean and straight, unlike her husband's handwritten stories about Việt Nam. He motions for Cam to sign her name next to the Xs on many different pages. When he hands the pen to her, it is the first time they have touched in months.

The apartments Cam applies for are smaller than some of the hotel rooms she cleans. Together, she and her growing baby learn the language of their new life.

When the girl no longer needs diapers and sleeps through the night, Cam begins graveyard shifts as a seamstress in a factory. These days of work leave her body more tired than it has been before.

Arriving home to the small bed they share, Cam nestles against her daughter's warm sleeping body and whispers to her memories of Việt Nam—the dog that she had when she was little, the smell of fried squid and the taste of salty air in Nha Trang, and the fog in Đà Lạt that made her skin so smooth. Cam rubs her face against her daughter's, breathing in the girl's skin and feeling the heat of her body radiate.

This is the last time they will be themselves. Like this.

~

The sun grows hotter as the boat approaches Thai waters. The old people have emerged from the stuffy hull to sit in the shade of the captain's bridge. The seamstress uses a fishing pole to lower her hand-sewn dresses into the water. Pulling them up dripping, she hands each one to a child to put across their foreheads. The dark girl sits in direct sunlight, edging her brown toes towards the young man with the uneven legs. He plays cards with her after they eat their daily rations. This young man playfully taps her white toenails. Even she is beautiful when she smiles.

Binh tries to catch fish to make up for the empty cháo pot. Since they left for Thailand, he has not been able to catch anything. He searches the water for other fishing boats that might be casting nets. Nothing. Soon they will have to eat the dry ramen noodles and hope for a summer rainstorm to replenish their water supply.

Binh's shoulders burn. His eyes tear from the brightness of sun against water.

He rests, leaning against the bow with the fishing pole. Binh fevers into a sleep and dreams of the fisherman's daughter in her dress white like the hot sun.

Binh is woken by the seamstress's protests. The fisherman is trying to stop her from waving her arms at an oncoming ship. "No," she cries as the fisherman wraps his strong arms around her, binding her own to her sides. "It's the flag. They see my flag. They will save us. We are lost."

"Shut your mouth," the fisherman says through his teeth. He wrestles her into the hull where she continues to shout. The fisherman ushers the old people and children below deck as well, leaving only the young man, the dark girl, and Binh in the sun with him. "Grab poles," he tells Binh and the young man who has grown to love the dark girl.

"You," the fisherman calls to her. "Clean something. Pretend you're Cambodian if you need to."

The fisherman squints at the ship's growing figure. It bears no nation's flag. It belongs to no waters.

~

Living in a small unit of a large apartment complex, Cam becomes only a mother, one of many adapting to America. The fluorescent lights in the supermarkets are so bright that she does not pocket the extra apple she feels she is owed for the price. She samples grapes instead, pushing one into her five-year-old daughter's mouth as the girl squirms in the seat of the shopping cart. In this country, people talk to the mother slowly. People think the mother is crazy or retarded or incapable of learning English. Frustrated that her daughter is not yet old enough to translate for her, the mother can only laugh at the holes and puckers that the Americans' mouths make. They turn to her wide-eyed daughter who appears to understand their language and tell her she looks like a doll. The girl smiles, not knowing this response will begin the slow separation between her and her mother.

The mother works two jobs but doesn't yet understand why her money is taxed before she can even finger the corners of dollar bills. She buys bellbottoms on sale and fake gold hoop earrings that her daughter tugs at when she is in her mother's arms. Together, the mother and daughter eat instant ramen noodles. A Mexican girl from an apartment upstairs suggests they try the noodles raw. When the mother is tired, they do. The mother tells her daughter that they can save more money by not flushing the toilet so much. She repeats the American words "dirty" and "yuck" and "no touch" at the little girl's wide eyes. In between shifts, the mother comes home to listen to the radio station that broadcasts names of boat people who have recently arrived and are looking for their families. As if exhausted by waiting for the name she never hears, the mother often falls asleep with the radio on. Waking from a nap one afternoon, the mother finds her toddler leaning in the toilet bowl, splashing the unclean water there.

~

A man who looks like the lead actor in one of Binh's favorite operas pushes him into line with the fisherman, the young man, and the dark girl with white toenails. He knocks the fishing poles from the three men's hands, not noticing that the line is missing from Binh's

37

pole as it slides across the deck.

The seamstress screams for help through the deck, her voice hoarse from thirst. The opera man yells something in Thai over his shoulder. As a man with decaying teeth from the Thai ship boards the boat, the soprano pirate clutches the fisherman's neck. The fisherman whispers in Vietnamese that they do not have anything, not even rice or water. When the pirate reaches in the fisherman's pocket and finds the bound wad of money intended for the Malaysian refugee camp authorities, he pries open the fisherman's mouth with a knife and cuts his tongue out. It drops to the deck between the fisherman's feet where it lies limp and thick and wet. The young man and Binh watch their captain sink to the deck and bleed.

The seamstress's cries from the hull cease.

The pirate on deck checks Binh's pocket and, finding them empty, rips the picture of his mother from the inside of his shirt. He licks his lips at the picture and shakes his head at Binh. He calls to the man below deck in Thai. The pirate with decaying teeth emerges from the hull wearing the gold and jade necklaces of the old women. He wipes his blood-spattered hands on the legs of his pants and walks, his eyes never shifting, to the dark girl.

Binh watches as the pirates bind ropes around the writhing legs and arms of the fisherman and the young man who loves the dark girl. She is looking to Binh to do something. She believes that the solider can save them. Her lover and the fisherman are laid face down on the hot deck. The young man calls to his dark girl, "You have to fight."

Seeing why he is not being tied up, Binh does not move except to shift the coil of fishing line in his mouth. He pretends to be scared for his life. The man with decaying teeth and the one who looks like he can sing tragedy each grab one of the dark girl's arms as she abides by her lover's request and kicks her legs, spits at the pirates. They only laugh at her as they pin her jerking body to the deck and undo their pants. The man with decaying teeth points at Binh with his knife and says in broken Vietnamese, "You like fuck ugly dark bitches, so you enjoy watch this."

In the war, Binh taught himself discipline. He learned to watch and wait, as he used to do during cricket fights in Đà Lạt. He feels that control again while watching the men rape the dark girl with white toenails. He allows them both to enter her. He permits her to stop fighting back. He scoots himself only an inch at a time across the deck as it tilts on rolling waves. He is close enough to the men now. The soprano clutches the girl's legs so hard as he fucks her that his fingertips make white marks on her skin. This man's face is turned to the sun. The man with decaying teeth sits on the girl's chest, cutting lines across her breasts. Between his knife and thumb, her plum-colored nipples are sliced off. The crying girl goes unconscious. In the moment before the men can grow bored with a body that does not struggle, Binh uncoils the fishing line from between his dry lips and pulls it tight around the soprano pirate's neck. Binh tugs back hard, pulling the man out of the dark girl and creating a line of blood across his neck. The man begins to choke as his partner rises from the girl's bloody chest and turns towards Binh.

Binh pushes the choking man overboard. He approaches the man with decaying teeth as he has many other men before. They fight. Binh feels the man's ribs dig into his body. He wonders how long this man has been at sea. Binh kills the man with his own knife. The body is dumped into a heaving wave.

Still tied up, the young man whimpers as blood from between his lover's legs slides down the deck towards him. Binh surveys the wide expanse of water around them.

There is silence.

~

At school, the daughter does not speak in class. She also does not enjoy recess. She spends much of it getting out of handball and tetherball lines to slurp from the arcs of water at the drinking fountain that is set away from the noise. The other girls in her class have named each of the four spigots iced tea, lemonade, soda pop, and pee, from left to right. Although this daughter does not like the girls or care to play with the new Chinese jump ropes their mothers have bought them, she never drinks from the pee fountain, making sure to remember that it switches to the left on opposite day.

On one particular day, the girl is thirsty and abandons an aggressive round of four square to drink iced tea. Mexican girls sucking on plastic containers of chili powder come up behind the girl as she is drinking and knee her in the butt, pour their spicy candy in her hair. The girl stops drinking but stays bent over the fountain, waiting for the girls to bore themselves and pass.

The fattest Mexican girl, though, drops an empty bag of Cheetos, ready to put her licked fingers to other uses. She grabs the girl's hair with her fat brown fingers and puts her round sweaty face next to hers. "Look at me, stupid," she says. The girl does not look, only focuses on the water that spirals down the drain of the drinking fountain. "What, puta," the fat girl says. "Can't you see me with your Chinese eyes?" The other Mexican girls chant, "Ching chong, ching ching chong."

With the fat Mexican girl's face panting next to hers, the daughter remembers something she once heard her mother scream at her father before he left. She repeats it, not knowing that she has told the round brown girl to go fuck some other whore. Her comment is met with silence, and, for a second, she thinks it has worked. "You stupid fucking chink," the fat Mexican girl says, her breath rank with the smell of cheese-flavored dust. She pushes the girl's face into the drinking fountain. The Mexican girl's arm is strong. The daughter walks, alone, to the nurse's office, holding a hand over her bleeding split lip. Once there, she hands the nurse her tooth and asks, "Can I call my mother?"

The phone only rings. The girl carries her tooth in a fist through the rest of the day, keeping her lips pressed together to conceal the empty space. When the school bell rings at the end of the day, the girl waits at the school's entrance where she can usually find her mother's face smiling from the passenger seat of a friend's car. Recently, her mother's drivers have been arriving later and later. The girl does not like the smell of these men's cologne.

The girl's patience having grown larger than herself, she waits. She presses the dirty imprint of her sneakers against walls; she adjusts and readjusts her backpack straps as other children are taken home; she kneels and drags her broken tooth across the sidewalk; she paces back and forth until the sun falls lazy. She decides to walk home and tosses what is left of her tooth into the street.

When she arrives, home is quiet and empty. The girl sits with a box of chocolate chip cookies that she hopes will combat the lingering smell of cologne in the small apartment. She waits.

~

The sun burns angry into the end of summer. Sweat and blood dry into wood. It darkens.

All of the bodies were dumped, the dark girl two days after she bled to death because her lover didn't want to let her go. Together, the young man and Binh have attempted to navigate the Pacific, letting the boat drift when the waves seem to push them in the right direction. They share the remaining dry ramen noodles.

Binh lies on the deck. His lips are crusted with salt, burned, and bloody. Having floated through only a few, brief rainstorms, Binh drinks his urine. His stomach has sunken. His vision is hazy. He and the young man do not bother speaking.

Waves move.  Time passes.
Worn of its color, the boat nudges a shore unfamiliar.

~

On a shore, the girl, now almost fully grown, meets the ocean again. Her mother told her once that she was born of the hour of this great body of water. A pack of barebacked boys sprints to the wave as it sprays up white, but reverse their formation before water settles into foam. She wonders what man her mother has left her for today.

The girl digs her toes into the wet sand. The water is cold here. In Việt Nam, her mother has reminisced, the water is warm. Regardless of its lack of borders, water, in her mother's language, means nation, is self. Tapping her tongue against salty lips, the girl stands out of waves' reach and searches for signs of herself in the ocean

Chad Tsuyuki

# Part Five: Nửớc-Nation

It is an eleven-hour bus ride from Sài Gòn to Nha Trang, the coastal city where my grandmother lived and worked during the U.S.-Việt Nam War. On the bus, we pass through miles of a countryside that gets postcarded to other parts of the world—endless rice paddies punctuated by conical rice hats, oxen crossing dirt roads. But, in every town we pass through, there are also coffin stores with infant-sized caskets in the front display and billboards with spray-painted hands and skulls and a few simple words: AIDS. Dangerous. Stop.

During the bus ride I feel the borderlands of Việt Nam/America creeping in, receding, encroaching, shifting. A young Saigonese boy sitting in front of me sings "We Wish You a Merry Christmas" (it is the middle of June) and his older sister, clad in Dolce and Gabana, chimes in for the chorus. It is this boy sitting in front of me who keeps me occupied for much of the eleven hours, his little legs kicking at the ceiling of the bus to the rhythm of his English language songs. I took a picture of one of his little outstretched legs. It is the only picture I took of a stranger in Việt Nam.

At lunchtime, the bus pulls into a truck stop, where a double amputee is sitting at the bottom of the bus's stairs with his stumps outstretched. As soon as I have registered his body, or what was left of it, I force my eyes to unfocus at a point beyond him and never meet his eyes. At the time, I justified doing this because I wanted to show the man that I did not treat him as any different than anyone else, and probably too to prove to everyone around me that such realities were familiar to me. I was trying to prove, more to myself, that this was my homeland and I knew it well enough not to notice.

I was arrogant. Anger rose in my throat as I watched a trio of Australian college girls from the back of the bus shuffle quickly past the man as he begged them for money. I had done the same. I knew

44

nothing. I wrestled with how to give the man money or a sandwich from the roadside stand without apologizing for ignoring him the first time around. While Chad ordered food for himself, I went to the bathroom and peed on my foot while squatting over the hole in the ground. I walked past a fly-covered rim of a jar of pickled duck eggs and, for the first time in Việt Nam, felt sick to my stomach. I never gave the man anything. We never met eyes. When it came time to get back on the bus, the man was seated on a bench smoking a cigarette. Back on the bus, the driver blasted a radio station playing a mix of Lady Gaga and traditional Vietnamese opera. The homeland I was searching for was a place that America never left.

# Phật Bà

When I was still young in body, my mother showed me how to place fruit and tiny cups of water for Phật Bà. This is the Vietnamese name for the Buddha who is also known as Quan Yin (or Guanyin) in China and Kannon in Japan, where she was the patron Buddha for immigrant sailors, largely in the 7th and 8th centuries as Buddhism spread in East Asia. Unmoored from home and riding the tides, these sailors prayed to her in her representation of compassion, acceptance, protection.

Growing up in my mother's attempts of creating a sense of home, Phật Ba's altar sat on top of the record player where the Alvin and the Chipmunks Christmas album lay spin-less under the broken needle. "She watches over us and our home, so she must eat and drink before we do," my mother told me. She guided my hand to pyramid the mandarin oranges, placing at the apex the one with a leaf curling from its stem.

"She eats and drinks..." I murmured. I looked at the Buddha's porcelain face, concentrating on her Mona Lisa smile painted in a thin pink line—this hue of life. I tried to imagine it opening wide in a pink 'O' for a big bite of tiny hamburger, or being licked by a little porcelain tongue hungry for deposits of residual ketchup and mustard. "How does she eat?" I asked. "And when? At night? Will she save some for us?" My mother's eyes smiled at me, which only made me anxious because she was not taking this seriously enough. "Does she get up and walk around too, Mom? Do you think she can climb onto my bed? Would she crawl into my mouth while I'm sleeping? Mom? How come you're not answering me? Would she?"

"Toi đi, con," my mother said in exasperation, shooing me away. As she returned to the kitchen to unload the rest of the groceries, my mother called over her shoulder, "She do, how you say? In-vis-i-bi-li-ty." (My mother has always enjoyed showcasing her skills with multisyllabic words in English.) Of course, I understood her beyond the sound of this word. I felt invisibility deeply. It was what I became when my mother was sad beyond comprehension, when her eyes did not seem to recognize my face. It was when my mother told me that she was going to stop taking pictures of me and stop celebrating my birthday when my baby teeth started falling out. And she did. It was, too, when everyone and everything that had happened in Việt Nam filled the space of our little apartment in San Pedro, California—unseen, yes, but undeniably present.

I remained standing in front of the altar. My eight-year-old belly bulged in Phật Bà's direction. She was still. I squeezed my eyes shut, imagining happy things—Disneyland, horses, Popsicles, hamburgers with spongy buns and wilted pickles, and then, helplessly, I pictured her porcelain arms emerging from the folds of her robe, the tink-tink of porcelain feet tapping down the hall toward my bedroom, Shaolin monk-kicking my teddy bear sentry into submission, her cold limbs goosebumping spots of my skin while it is warm with sleep, her closed yet all-seeing eyes peering into my dreaming face, her mockingly orange-scented breath on my cheek. (I think my dad had recently shown me the 1987 horror film *Dolls*.)

My heart pounding, my eyelids heavy with fear, I forced my eyes open.

Phật Bà was still motionless. A moment of relief. But, no. Motionless could be patience. She was waiting. Plotting. My body bursted into a run. In my bedroom, I barricaded myself with stuffed animals and my recently released Mexican Barbie, Nina, whose smooth plastic body I hoped could ward off any threatening non-corporeal forces.

Over the next day or two, my courage was fleeting yet explosive. Periodically, I jumped into the living room with "Ah-has!"

and an accusatory, elbow-locked point at Phật Bà. I never caught her in the act of eating, only my mother who, startled by one of my dramatic entries, flung her chopsticks into the air, scattering phở noodles and shreds of chicken from her soup bowl all over the coffee table where we sat cross-legged to eat every meal. "Troi đat oi, cái con nay," my mother cursed me, and I saw her lips tighten in anger under big  droplets of chicken broth that had splattered on her face. She picked up her chopsticks, shook them menacingly above her head, and chased me down the hall to my room where her anger, and my fear, subsided. A tickle fight ensued. I think I peed my pants during this skirmish, though, and my mother's lips tightened again and remained that way until she shouldered my bed sheets from the laundromat back to our apartment.

From then on, I adopted more subtle tactics of surveillance. With several stuffed animals and Nina in tow, I slowly approached the altar with bated breath. This silent approach did not fool Phật Bà either. Each time, she was still and patient. Nevertheless, I noticed that the oranges softened and the water levels in her tiny cups gradually sunk. I did not understand her voodoo magic, but I kept her in the corner of my eye as my mother an I watched *Melrose Place*, reruns of *Three's Company*, and Hitchcock movies. While she cursed Sydney, laughed at Jack and Mr. Furley or clicked her tongue and mumbled "ngu" at Chrissy, and practiced pronouncing the "er" sound in "birds," I watched Phật Bà.

At school, a science-based assembly kept my classmates and I squirming as the salty smell of tater tots wafted into the auditorium from the adjacent cafeteria. Anthropomorphized versions of biology concepts emerged in costume, singing and dancing across a cardboard set. Sitting behind me, my childhood love Joshua Mathews punctuated each musical number with a "Ha!" or "Dumbass tree!"

During a particular boring musical interlude about a sapling, Josh whispered, "Hey, Jade." I turned to him.

His eyes, always squinty under his unmanageable tuft of blonde hair, were squintier with smile crinkles, and he was fidgeting with the hems of his shorts as he always did when he was excited about something. He cleared his throat and announced, "Yo mama is so old, she's as old as the crust on your underwear." He immediately proceeded to nudge and jostle his friend Michael next to him, saying, "Oh, snap, that's messed up, Mike," as if silent, awkward Michael had come up with that "yo mama" joke.

The girls next to me looked at my crotch as if they will somehow see crusty underwear there on the outside of my jeans. They cringed and shifted away from me in their seats. I rolled my eyes and responded with a "*Your* mom" at Josh just to play along, but I turned back to the assembly with a smile on my face. This is how we pretended to deny what was real in our young hearts because we felt we had time enough.

Beyond that, my memory of the assembly is a blur—that is, until Ricki the Raindrop took the stage. A blue and furry man-sized raindrop, Ricki sang a song about how he rises and falls. In a duet with the sun, Ricki sang about the water cycle: "Solid. Sha na na. Liquid. Sha na na. Gasssss." Over Josh's heckling—"Dude, Mike, there's an actual guy in that stupid thing!"—all I could hear was one word echoing in my head: evaporation.

That afternoon in Latchkey, my disillusionment rendered me quiet and withdrawn. Careful as he was in his boyish love for me, Josh kept his distance, probably because he thought I was upset about the crusty underwear joke. Of course, I wasn't. He was, after all, the boy I was going to marry, so my forgiveness with him was boundless. While I drew misshapen horses in the margins of my multiplication tables homework, Josh slid a Rickey Henderson baseball card across the desk to me. "Thank you," I said. "No big deal, it's a duplicate," he responded. When my mom picked me up at twilight, Josh and I mumbled good-byes in the way that feeling, yet uncertain, children do.

When I got home, I dropped my backpack at the door and shuffled, eyes cast down, over to the record player. My mother mistook this defeated trudge of the newly science-minded for spiritual reverence and comes up behind me, resting her hand on my protruding belly. "Lay, Phật Bà, đi," she said, urging me to pray. She pressed her body against my back to make me bow. I stiffened in refusal. I didn't look at Phật Bà. "I show you," my mother said, taking my hands and pressing their palms together. She cupped my elbows and gently raised them up, then down, in the motion of prayer. "See? Not too bad." She handed me an orange from the altar.

"How did Phật Bà drink all of this?" I asked, giving my parent a second chance, as children are still open-hearted enough to do.

"I tol' you," she replied, annoyed.

"Well," I said, putting the orange back on the pyramid, "a fuzzy man-sized raindrop told me about evaporation today. That's where the water goes, Mom. Not in Phật Bà. To the sky." I crossed arms across my belly.

My mother, exasperated, clicked her tongue. She has never liked when I tell her about school. She feels I am talking down to her, spotlighting her shortcomings. (I learn to tell her nothing about my degrees in English, although when I get to my PhD, I mention that I am writing my dissertation about Vietnamese writers. She hesitated, then lifted her chin and told me, "I live that. I no have to read about it." To cement me in my place, she added, "No man want marry PhD girl.")

"Let me tell you," she said, her lips tight, and my body tensed awaiting punishment. She switched to Vietnamese and her eyes travelled far away. I knew that the invisibility was taking over again. "When I was little, like you," and she momentarily looked at, and saw, me, her daughter—flesh, blood, and memory, "I was playing at the lake in Đà Lạt. I never went all the way in because I don't know how to swim, but I was splashing with my feet." Here, she reenacted the movements of her girlhood body, and I longed to befriend my mother when we were both just little girls. I wondered if I would be able to recognize her. After all, it seems that most stories hinge upon the moment of recognition—the hero unmasks the villain; a parent encounters the future in the child's quick, searching eyes; longtime friends confess the full depths of their formerly inhibited hearts to each other...

"Hot!" She switched back to English to emphasize the point to me, her foreign child. "It were so hot!" She continued, but in Vietnamese: "Many of the townspeople had gathered lakeside to cool off, and I could see people fishing and some boys on the banks were flying kites. But I was by myself." She was, as in so many of her stories, alone. "I was watching the boys' kite fly when my eyes travelled further upward, to the sky." At this point, I was afraid that my girl-mother sees a plane and that this story will add to the staggering body count that her other tales have already tallied. My mother's eyes gazed upward, where I only see the cottage cheese texture of our apartment ceiling. "And there was Phật Bà!"

"Wait—"

But my mother talked over my attempted interjection. "It was as if the ripples of heat were the folds of her robe," she said. I looked to the altar beside us where the porcelain figure was cold to the touch. I turned back to my mother and listened: "Her face was so beautiful, filling the sky. Her eyelids were still heavy, but it was as if she was looking at me, as if she could see only me. And then she raised one of her arms and pointed. She pointed me to the hills." My throat was dry, the anticipation unswallowable.

My mother continued, "Something told me to run. So I ran. I ran and left my sandals at the lake. I ran as fast as I could toward the hills, until my chest was burning and my legs were like rubber. It was while I was running that the air raid sirens began to scream. So I ran with my hands over my ears. I made it to my grandmother's house, where she smacked me for being outside while the sirens were sounding, but I knew she did it because she was relieved I was home. She pushed me away from the windows, and I lay on the hard-packed dirt floor of the kitchen to let my body cool. From the loudspeakers, a Northern Vietnamese accent told us that we were under twenty-four-hour curfew. So I lay there for that night, and about six more days after that. We heard gunfire in the distance. We ran out of rice, so my brothers and I ate bugs that crawled into the house." I could envision my uncles doing this for sport, but when I pictured my mother catching bugs, it was a delicate process of waiting, cupping her hands, and tenderly plucking the legs and antennae from insects' bodies. I imagined because I know the tenderness of my mother's heart, that she felt guilty for taking so much from these bugs, simply trying to live. "We survived," my mother said. "That is how Phật Bà saved me. She brought me home."

My mother's eyes regained their focus and finally registered my face. When she looked at me, she said to me, in English, "Don't cry. You ugly when you cry."

I wouldn't be writing this if it were a story of irreparable disillusionment, or a finite reconciliation of my faith and my formal education. Things don't work linearly or neatly like that. Sometimes the intensity of prayer wracks me with tears or when I see a certain bird I'm overcome by the presence of my great aunt. Other times, I walk by Phật Bà where she sits on the altar I have made in my own home with the same suspicion and detachment I felt after that assembly in the third grade. Since that day, I have learned that I possess invisible knowledges and the knowledges that are in print; they are not always mutually exclusive.

I lost touch with Joshua Mathews after my mother abruptly decided to move the summer before sixth grade. So, we never married as my young heart had planned. Years later, in college, I found out that Josh died in his early twenties, of what I still do not know.

Phật Bà came to me in dreams for the first time in years, but not in the way that she has for my mother. I dream I am on the playground of my elementary school. It is twilight but children are outside playing, skipping through jump-ropes and kicking a soccer ball. The collar of a brown cotton sweatshirt brushes against my lips and suddenly I am aware of my body. I am inside this huge brown sweater with Josh. Though it covers the two of our child bodies fully, our limbs are tangled up together, as we pull each other closer and closer in this cotton cocoon. I turn and look at his face. It appears to me clearly. His eyes squint at me and his lips press into a thin pink smile. I lean my cheek against his and find warmth there.

As she did for the sailors riding currents Japanward so long ago, and for the fear-stricken and lovely-hearted girl-mother of mine running toward life before I knew it, Phật Bà connects us, protects us from that dizzying orbit of feeling lost.

## Part Six: Beach-Brothel

The beach in Nha Trang is partially fenced off to prevent locals from entering sections of the coastline purchased by Chinese, Japanese, French, German resorts. The "open" stretches of the beaches are for sale too. Thatch-roof cabanas and jet skis are rented by the hour, restaurants sell french fries and cá kho on the same menu. The only South Vietnamese on the beach are the workers. The sharp pitch of the Northern Vietnamese dialect nearly indistinguishable to my ears, Hanoi businessmen lie under cabanas drinking 333 beers, talk on their cell phones, and check their Rolexes. Everyone else is English, Australian, French and sunburned. I sit among them in a bikini as a South Vietnamese woman, covered from head to toe, bears across her shoulders a yoke weighted with a basket of writhing lobsters on one end and a pot of boiling water on the other. She stops in front of us to set her load down. No one comes to buy lobsters. A police officer yells at her from across from the sand, demanding to see permits. From within her layers of clothing, she pulls out squares of laminated paper, and the officer pats the back of her knees with his baton to tell her to keep moving.

Swimming in the South China Sea, I am reminded of a photo taken of my grandmother, my aunt, and one of my uncles wading in the water on the very same stretch of beach. Floating there is comforting but I recognize that the setting is very different. The wildly overgrown islands in the background of that photo from the '60s have now been tamed and are dotted with billboards advertising Vin Pearl, the amusement park-style resort that has been built out there. One of the longest aerial trams in the world takes visitors from the mainland to the island. I do not pay for this ride. I swim and float in the water all day.

In the mornings, the sea welcomes me to where my inherited

memories were born.

In the afternoon, the undertow is strong and tires my legs quickly, reminding me that I do not belong there.

In the evening, Chad and I dinner at one of the seaside restaurants built specifically for tourists. I ached to go inland where I could pray to the giant marble Phật Bà at the monastery on the mountain, but I am also regretfully lured in by the seductive ease of the tourist areas. I am fatigued by the heat, my guilt, having to explain myself when people looked at me quizzically when I spoke Vietnamese to them. Shamefully, I am relieved when we set foot in the restaurant where the teak tables were sectioned off by man-made babbling waterfalls and tropical plants. For the first time on the trip, I do not try to communicate in Vietnamese. The back of the restaurant opened up onto the beach, where the sun was setting as a perfect backlight for Chad and I to take photos of our beers silhouetted by the dusky sky, like a Corona commercial. The setting reminds me of Mexico, so beautiful yet all the more unjust that it was cordoned off to the locals.

Around us, Korean businessmen raucously cheer on their teams in the World Cup, kicking off their shoes and toasting one another. Amid the celebratory noise, I notice by the water a table of brash, red-faced Australian men each with a young Vietnamese woman. The woman with a hard-lined face has a son who is sitting cross-legged under the table playing an old Gameboy. Occasionally, she nudges him and passes a handful of food under the table. Just as quickly, she turns back to who I assume is her john or prospective husband and gives him a coy "oh, baby" as he laughs and gets redder. I wonder if this is the way it was when my grandmother lived and worked here, save for the obnoxious Australian tourists replaced by American soldiers. I wonder if that boy under the table was ever one of my uncles. Chad and I eat our dinner, but I keep my eye on the table, and the boy beneath it. As we receive our dessert, I see that the boy's mother gets up and heads to the restroom. I excuse myself to follow her. I don't know why, if I'm trying to understand my grandmother better or to feel more connected to the realities undergirding the postcard settings of Nha Trang. I don't ask her any questions or speak to her at all. As we wash our hands at the side-by-side sinks, I glance up to see her inspecting her face in the mirror and then adjusting her top. She looks at her reflection matter of factly, and does not acknowledge that I am there.

Chad Tsuyuki

# Muscle and Memory

On August 2$^{\text{nd}}$, 2012, Vietnamese German gymnast Marcel Nguyen won a silver medal at the London Olympics in the men's Individual All-Around. As my overseas, mixed-Viet homeboy flew and flipped and swung, I thought, "that dude is *at work* right now." His career is dedicated to his body, training it to perform feats that showcase the human specimen at its most physically impressive. When I think of Marcel and possibility, I turn inward, to the point at which memory and muscle meet.

Athleticism was not at all an avenue of pursuit when I was growing up. That's not how I was raised to see my body, as being able to go above and beyond. It was about surviving.

When I told my mom that I wanted to join the girl's softball team in junior high and again in high school, she said, "No! So stupid ball break your face?" Sports were an unnecessary danger in a world my mother found to be so threatening and unpredictable as history had proven it to be. She added, "Why do you want to run when no one is chasing you?"

Before my mother (and, oh, my lack of coordination) dashed my childhood dreams of becoming an Olympic gymnast, I catapulted over the couch and attempted handstands on the coffee table (read: balance beam) until the cheap "wood" paneling clung to my sweaty palms. To the sight of her firstborn daughter's gangly legs launching airborne across her living room, my mother would quickly ground me with reminders of the household responsibilities we shared in being on our own and both being students. Cleaning. Homework. Alleviating each other's loneliness. Cooking. Eating. Eating. Surviving.

My mother used to get me to finish the food on my plate by telling me stories about her hunger in Việt Nam. On some days during the war-time curfews, she resorted to eating insects she spotted crawling around the house. Though enthralled by these stories of my mother as a girl-survivor, they began to ring empty for me. Despite growing up on welfare in a housing project and occasionally knowing hunger, I surely never had to eat bugs. So, my mother resorted to other tactics to ensure that food never went to waste. "If you eat this, I will love you," she only had to tell me once. And, for better or worse, this worked.

I ate and ate and continued to eat long after my mother and I no longer lived together, shared meals, or even talked. I ate through my loneliness for my mother, my string of pained relationships, the stress of a graduate degree and then another. I ate to celebrate in good times, in bad times to "reward" myself for simply getting through the day.

Once, for a short period of time during my teenage years, I swung in the opposite direction and stopped eating. My brother and sister were under five years old then, and I had become invisible, eclipsed by their cuteness, their new life and emerging potential. Now, I can see that was trying to be seen by my mother who had, until that point, been so attentive to food and how I ate. I began counting calories and lowering the ceiling more and more each day, to the point that I was down to a glass of juice and three crackers a day, all while I rode the exercise bike that usually sat dormant and dusty in my mom's house. My mother didn't notice. Desperate and weak, I was babysitting my sister one day and got up off the couch to chase her. I collapsed, knocking my head against the tiles. I woke up with my three-year-old sister hovering above me, confusion and worry on her little face. That's when I stopped depriving my body of food.

I started eating again to get my mother to love me, and I got too big to wear the dresses she and her consistently ninety-pound body deemed beautiful, too fat to attract a husband that her old-school values expected of me at age twenty-five. In feeling her disappointment in me, rather than her love, I began to instead eat for that reason, as if to spite her by getting so big my body no longer remotely resembled the figures of any of the Vietnamese women in my family, to get so big that the last time she hugged me, my mother remarked that I was "big" and "soft like a pillow." She reminds me that my collarbone cracked during birth because I was so big and she so small.

By the time I visited Việt Nam for the first time in 2010, I was at my heaviest. A picture from this trip shows my body, not effectively hidden by my intentionally baggy clothes, hanging heavy on the back of a motor scooter, eclipsing the body of the driver, my friend Vinh. From my hotel room window, I watched the elderly playing badminton in the park before the sun beat too hot and men balance a nap on top of their motorbikes.

At a tailor in Cho Lon (Sài Gòn Chinatown), a woman with soft skin offered to make me an áo dài. Without thinking, I told her I was too fat, that I eat way too much. I cringed inside, realizing the nasty American privilege of my statement. She responded, "That means you're well-fed, prosperous. That's a good thing. It's beautiful." She smiles and rubs my arm in a way that I feel a mother would. Nevertheless, I felt ashamed. And confused. I caught myself mid-twist in the oscillations of how to view my own body.

As the medals continue to be hung around bowed necks at the London Olympic Games, I push through the most excruciating exercise and diet regimen to which I have ever committed. Nausea and fatigue knot in my stomach even now as I visualize Jillian Michaels' disturbingly non-sweaty face as she drill sergeants me through painful squat thrusts and chest flies and other oh-my-god-I'm-dying exercises. I push through the pain in hope of achieving some (im)possible medium between my mother's skinny and her wishes for me to eat, eat for love. I know my mother would shake her head if she knew that I no longer eat white rice or the bánh bò or đậu hũ that I've loved ever for as far back as my taste buds anchor my memories. But, the generation of survivor that she is, she would be happy I'm (slowly but surely) slimming down to a single-digit clothing size to attract a potential husband. She forgets that I, generation of survivor that I am, take care of myself.

So when I watch Marcel Nguyen and the ridiculously impressive physical specimen that he is as he performs the world-class feats of the human body, I wonder about the possibilities of the body within our cultures, our memories. Will it be possible for me, as a Vietnamese American woman, to be happy with my body at any point? Will there be a day that my mother will be okay with the fact that my body was born of hers? What kinds of hunger will I foster in my children? How loudly will I scream from the stands?

I grapple with these yet unanswerable questions about this body I should know as my own, settling to watch the Olympic athletes' bodies on television and then inspect my slowly changing one in the bathroom mirror during commercial breaks. I found a picture of Marcel. In it, he is shirtless, and the tattoo across his chest reads, "Pain is Temporary, Pride is Forever."

Yes.

The pain of sweat and burn and food and hunger and war and survival and my mother's brand of love and feeling ugly in the dark and being the only Vietnamese Hidle and strengthening and of writing this at all. Of all the possibilities. The pain and the pride of tireless, inconceivable possibilities.

# Part Seven: North-South

Nha Trang is the furthest north that I travel. I do not bother crossing the 17$^{th}$ parallel because the border is everywhere in South Việt Nam.

There are the renamed streets, but for me this is not a firsthand loss—all of the streets are disorienting in their newness, and I learn to edge across them to the rhythm of the traffic.

There are the KFCs with statues of Colonel Sanders that have been modified to look more like Uncle Ho. American corporations lay claim to many corners in the cities, proof that South Việt Nam is being bought and sold every day. In the memoir of his first return to Việt Nam, Andrew X. Pham writes, "My Saigon is a whore. [...] Everything is for sale."

There are the bodies disfigured by war—chemical burns that have melted faces, explosives that have disappeared arms and legs—and the jokes some South Vietnamese tell about dirty Northerners being "too Chinese."

The gardens of the War Remnants Museums display North Vietnamese tanks and planes with crossed out South Vietnamese flags on their tails. There is also an outdoor exhibit featuring a tiger cage and other torture devices accompanied by placards describing which officers were tortured during the war. It is often unclear to me who is Northern and who is Southern. Sometimes the histories on the placards seem unsure themselves. Back in Little Saigon, California, my mother was always sure to explicitly point out to me which streets not to walk down or shop on because that is where the "rich North Vietnamese," she would say, "buy up all of the land and buy their way into our schools." On different streets history repeats.

Inside, where history is constructed, one of the exhibits juxtaposes photographs of the deformed bodies of napalm victims with excerpts from the U.S. declaration of independence. An English woman next to me comments on the horror of this hypocrisy laid bare. For a moment I admit, silly and shameful, that I consider imitating her accent for the remainder of my visit to the museum, as if that will somehow absolve my guilt by association, as if taking on an English side of history is more decided because its wounds feel more distant, less raw.

As part of the ongoing celebrations of the thirty-fifth anniversary of the Fall of Saigon, or what is officially called Reunification in Việt Nam, a parade of boats float along the Saigon River at night, the surface of the murky water reflecting the multicolored lights and sparklers that attempt to mimic the explosions of war. On the banks of the river, a few small children wave the flag of the Republic of Việt Nam, not the South Vietnamese flag whose three red stripes, my mother always stressed to me, represented the unity of the three regions of Việt Nam . "Three?" I'd asked her. "The central region of Hué," she explained to me in Vietnamese, "is where the ancestors of all of us, Southern and Northern, come from. A long time ago, we once had kings and queens who ruled the whole country from Hué. But the palaces were destroyed long ago and, so, people forget."

# Disease in Dialogues

The first doctor is a tiny brown Filipino woman. When she enters, she looks up from my chart at my mother who is standing in the corner of the room clutching her purse as she always does in new places. "Yade?" she says to my mother.

"No, that's me," I say. "And it's Jade. Hard 'J'." The doctor glances back at the chart, then back at me, and then back to the chart. "Oh," she says. As she untangles her stethoscope, I see her give me a once over, checking my clothes and posture, I guess, for some indication of promiscuity or drug use. "You're so young," she says and listens to my heart. I see my mother wince. I am not sure if the doctor's comment is made out of concern or condemnation, so I merely say "yes."

"Inhale," the doctor orders, so I hold in a deep breath as her stethoscope listens to the body beneath my shoulder blades and underneath my ribs.

"Lie back," the doctor tells me as she turns away to scribble on my chart. This is the first of countless afternoons I will spend with the tissue on the examination table clinging to my sweaty back.

"Lift up your shirt," she says, miming the motion for me. The woman lays one of her child-sized hands over the other and presses into my exposed belly, pushing under the ribs, kneading my right side until it feels like bruising. I can see my mother, still in the corner, craning her neck slightly to see where this doctor touches me, or maybe to see how her daughter's body has changed since she last saw it in my childhood.

"Inhale. Hold it." The woman's fingers dig under my ribs, and I focus on the buzzing of the fluorescent lights. My breathing feels obscenely loud.

The woman turns back to my chart, leaving me on the table with my belly exposed and without instruction. Once I sit up, she opens her eyes wide and over-enunciates every word that is not a command. "Hepatitis is a disease of the liver," she says. I don't understand why this is her starting point. Attached to my chart are blood tests from the Vietnamese clinic where I tested positive for Hepatitis B. I shoot a sideways glance at my mother and she looks both confused and insulted. "When the liver gets sick..." This is when I tune out her Sesame Street rendition of diagnosing chronic diseases and focus on her drawn-in eyebrows, as she is instructing me on the basics of my body.

I think of my grandmother's eyebrows, of how in pictures from the sixties they were drawn in dark and heavy. Back then, my grandmother caked on make-up to whiten her skin and darken her features, teased her hair into beehives, and boasted a gold tooth that surely attracted the men who chose her: the French expats who remained in Việt Nam after their country's government had retreated, Chinese businessmen who had come to make a profit off of the South, and the native Vietnamese men whose memories wrenched them away from the beds they shared with their wives and children.

Maybe it is the blood of one of these faceless men that runs through my mother's veins. And mine. It is the moment when this man's fingers first touched my grandmother's milk skin under the blue glow of a neon bar sign that I am vomiting bile in a high school bathroom. It is the slide of this man entering my grandmother's body with a shuddering breath when I am, at sixteen, overcome with a hardness and heat pressing against my right rib cage that I have to walk out of school early, carrying this weight, and tell my mother, to whom I barely ever speak, that I need to get tested for what I thought was *her* disease.

The little Filipino woman's eyebrows have relaxed over eyes more serious: "...should not have more than 1,000, but you have

68

forty-nine million of this virus living in your liver. You have to be very careful not to infect someone." Suddenly, the words are slow and I can see only one at a time. *Infect.* I think of zombies and evacuations and hazmat suits. "No more sex. No more needles." *More?* I don't bother to look at my mother. I feel guilt and shame for the sex I haven't had, the drugs I haven't done, merely for the fact that my mother has to listen to this and take it as truth from a woman she would usually push out of the way with her cart at the grocery store.

"Very important," the doctor says, and I look up at her face, a floating dark circle in a room of sanitized, blinding white. "Do not expose anyone to your feces. Very. Infectious." I stifle my bewildered laugh because the doctor seems very pleased with the dramatic gravity of this final statement. She smiles at me, my mother, and with my chart clutched to her chest, leaves us without further instruction.

"Mom, did she just tell me not to throw my poop at people? Like a monkey?"

The corner of my mother's mouth twitches with smile but she quickly waves her hand through the air and clicks her tongue in irritation as we walk out of the office. I fear that she will be irritated with me for wasting her afternoon, but she surprises with me with one of her rare yet fierce moments of protectiveness, perhaps borne of guilt. A flood of words having built up during her silence in the exam room, she releases: "Mấy cái bà Filipino này don't no know nothing. Nói với my daughter không có chổi với cúc được, huh? Feces? Why you do that? Bác sĩ này không biet di hết. Bà không cho nố medicine, no nothing. Chác phải đi bác sĩ Việt. You know," and here she clutches my elbow and my scalp tingles with the unfamiliarity of it, "Mẹ saw an ant crawling on the table in there. In Vietnamese place, okay, but here, no. Gê quá! Come, let go get some Vietnamese food and Chinese herbal. Make you feel lot better." My mother shuffles in her sandals ahead of me to the car. When she unlocks the passenger side door for me, she turns back and squints at me through the sunlight. "See, con? We take care ourselves."

At home, my mother pulls out a spoon.

Now, for most American children, spoons are for scooping ice cream and fishing the marshmallows out of Lucky Charms cereal. But, for me, the spoon is, too, a wince-inducing instrument bearing along its rim a layer of oil and flakes of my bloodied skin.

My mother nudges me until I lie facedown on the couch where she rolls up my shirt and unhooks my bra. Her palms, hot with the stinging odor of eucalyptus oil, rub my back. When her hands pull away momentarily, I grip the arm of the couch, inhale, and hold it as the edge of the spoon begins to scrape up, down, and along my ribs. I have never been able to speak during this process, not because it is the most painful thing, but because I know this is one of the few times that she can feel most like my mother. I do not want to take that away from her.

"You see?" my mother says. "All the bad, cold wind come out. Too cold." She tells me the same thing every time she performs the cạo gió ritual on me.

My mother explains that everything has a temperature. "Xoài...you understand?"

"Mmmm hmmm," I nod into the bed, too uncomfortable to bother reminding her that she was, after all, the one who had taught me Vietnamese. She translates the word into English anyway. "Mango," she starts with because she knows I love the fruit, "rất là nóng. Eat too much make body hot." And, as if to be fair, she tells me that the soymilk I also love is okay to drink while sick. "Cool down," she nods in approval.

She scratches extra hard on the skin. I squeeze my eyes shut. From the couch where my mom is scraping away at my back, I finally look up at Phật Bà's porcelain face. I want to feel the power and wonder of the Phật Bà's in my mother's stories. When she appeared vast and glowing in the heat-rippled sky on the first day of Tết Mậu

70

Thân in 1968, ushering my mother indoors to escape the infiltrating Việt Cong. Or how when my mother was pregnant with my sister, Phật Bà appeared in her dreams, like a hazy warm outline. I want to feel that, to see it, but she is unchanged, unflinchingly still—indifferent to me. That is why the Phật Bà my mother brought back from Việt Nam for me usually goes neglected through multiple cycles of the moon—her water cups dry out and I eat fruit without even thinking to offer some to her first.

My mother says, "Mom and Phật Bà want you die like you born." She touches my skin. "Everything here. Stay inside." She digs the spoon into each of my shoulder blades and drags it down the sides of my back. "Xông," she announces, finally finished, and rubs one final palmful of eucalyptus oil into my red and raw skin. I can feel the heat in the shape of her hand.

# Part Eight: Home

It is not until I am on my way back to the U.S. that someone welcomes me home to Việt Nam. On the flight back to the U.S. that connects in Taiwan, I sit next to an old woman who is wrapped in blankets and scarves, and clutches her purse to her chest. Halfway through the flight, the toddler in the row in front of us begins jumping and singing, peering his head between the seats to look at us. I make funny faces at him, which only makes him laugh and jump up and down more.

The old woman next to me, silent up until that point, clicks her tongue and leans into me. She is the first person during the whole trip to immediately, unquestioningly speak Vietnamese to me without hearing me speak Vietnamese first. "This little boy is such a trouble-maker. Children have no values anymore." While I feel bad for the boy, who I think has been pretty well behaved for three-hour flight, I am swelling with the comfort of this woman assuming I am Vietnamese and including me in her old-school values. So I agree with her that he is a brat. The boy's mother overhears, pushes him down into his seat, and tightens the seatbelt.

This pleases the old woman and she begins to ask me where I travelled in Việt Nam. I tell her that I only travelled to the cities where my family came from, and this old woman, who has lived through two wars, does not spend a second analyzing my face to figure out how Vietnamese came to look like me. I want to embrace her for this unquestioning acceptance.

The woman and I chat for awhile before the captain announces that we are beginning our descent into Taiwan. The woman adjusts her purse and tightens the handkerchief tied in a knot under her chin. I wish her safe travels, luck, and good health. "Thank you, child,"

73

she says. "And welcome home."

Nearly a full day of travel later, I arrive at my mother's house in Garden Grove, California. My younger brother opens the door looking all of his sixteen years in basketball shorts and messy bedhead in the afternoon. (I've asked him before if he carries Việt Nam and the war with him, and he does not hesitate to answer "no." He explains that it's not his country, not his experience, and he does not really think about being Vietnamese because there are a string of other Nguyens and Phams and Trans in his yearbook.) I embrace him as he, in teenage fashion, stands there stiff with his arms at his sides and probably embarrassed that his older sister clings to him. He does not ask me what our family's country was like, or how the 18-hour flight was, nor does he say that he is happy to see me safe and sound. All he says is, "You smell like Việt Nam." I smile into his shoulder because I know I am home.

J ade Hidle holds an MFA in creative writing from CSU Long Beach and a PhD in literature from UC San Diego. She is a faculty member in the Letters Department at MiraCosta College. As a featured writer for the Diasporic Vietnamese Artists Network's website, diacritics.org, she contributes articles on topical issues in Vietnamese art and culture, as well as essays about her experiences growing up as a second-generation, mixed-race Vietnamese in Southern California. Her work has also appeared in the *New Delta Review, International Journal of Comic Art, Spot Literary Magazine, Beside the City of Angels:  An Anthology of Long Beach Poetry, Word River,* and *The Ethnic Studies Review.*